This Book Belongs to:

____

www.ingramcontent.com/pod-product-compliance
Lightning Source LLC
Chambersburg PA
CBHW052115020426
42335CB00021B/2772
9781997510079